I0482115

INTRODUCTION TO ENTREPRENEURIAL SKILLS II

Kayode Asoga-Allen

© **K. ASOGA ALLEN**

First published 2015

ISBN: 1535246545

www.kayodeasogaallen.com

DEDICATION

This book is dedicated to Almighty God, the giver of knowledge, the Creator of heaven and earth and all that are in it, Omnipotent, Omnipresent and Omniscience, for making it possible for me to make exploit on earth.

No one can receive anything on earth except it is given to him from heaven; I am grateful to God for considering me worthy and destined me among those who will make impact in this world. Human beings have tried to put the light off, but this light is from God therefore, it is unquenchable. Glory and honour be to His holy name.

Praise God, Halleluiah.

PREFACE

The course "Entrepreneurial Skills" was introduced into the curriculum of Nigerian higher institutions of learning to proffer solution to the problem of unemployment facing the graduates of our higher institutions. Unemployment has become a national issue today in Nigeria; graduates of many years who have not tested any work are found everywhere. Most of these graduates have no skill in any occupation, thus they found it difficult to earn a living.

In most advanced countries of the world, the government has the statistics of yearly admissions into the higher institutions as well as yearly output of graduates. This enables the government to pursue vigorously the creation of jobs for the graduates. In Nigeria, that is not the case, the government at all levels seems not to bother whether graduates from our institutions are employed or not. No wonder, millions of Nigerian youths are jobless.

The economy of the nation, if well managed, is capable of providing employment for all the citizens, but politics is an impoverish game, the way it's played in Nigeria. The focus of most Nigerian politicians is how to corruptly enrich oneself.
Some past rulers of the nation are richer than even the nation that they ruled. Thus, politics is do or die in Nigeria,

because politics is the only business you can do to become overnight millionaire and billionaire. The level of corrupt practices of Nigerian politicians has created a serious problem of unemployment, poverty and penury for the citizens.

It is believed that with the introduction of this course "Entrepreneurial skills" students would be imparted with the skills necessary for establishing their own businesses after graduation, and be less dependent on government for a job. This book titled "Introduction to Entrepreneurial skills" have been written to cater for the students and general public who wish to become successful businessman and woman also, who desires to become an employer of labour in future rather than waste scarce time looking for unavailable job.

The content and ideas contained in this book would be of innumerable and inestimable value to the readers, most of the examples originated from the practical experience of the author as someone who has lectured the course for more than six years. Thus, I congratulate both the students of this course and the general public for the emergence of new ideas in the field of entrepreneurship.

Wishing all the prospective readers of this book, the best in their endeavours.

Kayode Asoga-Allen
B.A.(Ed.), M.Ed. Ph.D in view

Table of Contents

CHAPTER ONE: CASH PLANNING AND CASH CONTROL

Introduction

Cash can be defined in several ways. Ordinarily, it can be defined as money or money's worth with which your indebtedness to a third party can be universally settled. On the philosophical level, Yoruba's define cash as "the thing in hand which is the grandfather of confidence and arrogance, the thing not at home, which is the grandfather of fear and trembling".

However defined, cash is an expendable, wasteable but crucial resource which is mostly likely to be expended or wasted, by someone, somewhere, sometime, and somehow, unless someone, somewhere, sometime, somehow effectively says "no" by asking why? When? How? Who? Where? Or what? Or a combination of same.

The purpose of cash planning is to ensure that cash or cash acceptable equivalent is available when you want, in the right quantity at the right time and in the right place.

From Feasibility to Operating Budgets

Whenever possible, the feasibility projections, which you prepared or was prepared by experts for your projects, should constitute the nucleolus of your cash planning system. To this end, it is quite practicable to open your ledgers along the layout of your proposed expenditures. To do this, you would transfer to the page for the particular head of expenditure say "land and building" the amount which you projected on to the right hand corner in red ink and rule off with two lines. As you make the daily or monthly expenditure on "land and building" they would be cumulated under a column called "cumulative actual" this will be followed by a column called "projection balance" which is purely memoranda. In this way you would quickly begin to have advance warnings of "cost over-run" the single most deadly enemy of all new projects. If the project has not gone half way physically and the actual expenditure exceeds 60% you have an early warning signal of financial trouble ahead.

You should render such a comparison on all headings of your project's cost categories and keep a vigilant watch over every one of the items. Where costs are running away on any item you should find effective ways of controlling such including making effective savings on other headings. Should such compensating saving not be feasible or desirable, you would be wise to begin to explore the possibilities for raising additional money long before the need actually arise.

Among the possibilities, you should consider in this order:

a.   Realizing your cash savings, if any
b.   Selling some personal inessentials
c.   Raising money from friends and associates
d.   Raising money from all possible relations
e.   Raising money from banks
f.   Raising money from insurance companies and other finance institutions, or
g.   Enlisting additional shareholders occasioning some loss of control or delusion of authority.

Limiting cost over-runs

Immediately you observe the first signs of disruption in any one item of your feasibility projections, you should immediately take steps to review the entire feasibility projections, realistically in the light of prevailing and forecastable circumstance. You would then know the full extent of your possible resources gap, decide quite early, what chance you have of completing the project without unbearable or excessive strain. Sometimes, it may be better to abandon and sell off cost over-run projects, than to vainly or hopelessly pour in more resources, only to abandon it in the end.

Also, such timely and compressive cost and finance review will prevent you from making adhoc financial arrangements, too often, and too inadequately. Such exercises erode confidence in your judgment, destroy hopes for the project, and embarrass all those who might have been willing to be of genuine help.

Cost over-run is the single most common feature of all government sponsored abandoned projects.

Controlling Operating Costs

Having planned your project's cash requirement through a soundly prepared feasibility report, you have since taken steps to raise the necessary money for the project-investor's, shareholding investor loans; suppliers' deferred credits, private loans and bank loan. It is now time to commence operations.

Again the basis of control is the feasibility report. As in the case of the capital costs, the objective of cash planning, here is to ensure that you would have at least the right amount of money at the right place, and at the right time to pursue the predetermined production and selling activities so as to achieve the profit level envisaged in the feasibility projections or better.

Ideally the figures in the feasibility forecasts should constitute your operating budget. However because of the time lag that usually occurs between a project's conception and its realization, you would do well to examine the operating forecasts afresh, and bring them in line with reality. Such an exercise will show you the probable feature courses of actions.

For instance, a Nigerian promoted bakery project in Kwara State, but by the time production was to start, the cost of flour which account for 40% of total cost had changed from N18 a bag to N100. So also had all other input costs. Soon, the overdraft of N250,000 which the entrepreneur had arrange was soon swallowed up. Selling prices could not be raised except marginally. Switching facilities to chin chin did not provide volume or much respite and before long, the project folded up. Faced with alarming bank loans and overdrafts, worried and sleepless, the Tycoon fell ill and had to be hospitalized for months.

Thus not only do you have to have adequate cash to pursue your operations, your affairs must be arranged that your costs subtracted from sales receipt leave ample margined to services your debts.

In cash planning, therefore effective budgetary control system that compared your monthly budget or cost allocation on each class of expenditure for one month, against the actual expenditure for the month, yielding a "surplus" or a "shortage"

Similarly, you should compare the actual against the month's planned sales extra the favourable or unfavourable variance from plan.

Wherever possible, you should sell on a cash and carry basis. But where you have to sell on credit you have to make sure.

a. That you investigate the prospective customer quite properly. If possible, ask your bank manager to make discrete enquiry from the customer's bank. Bank can usually exchange more realistic information, than you can ever get yourself.

b. That you are not dazzled by the customers who showers you with lot of large deposits to start with, only to lure you into false sense of security and dupe you by taking more and more credits later.

c. That you set a level either to the amount or to the number of months for which you can give customer credit. Stick to the level by all means. In credit matters it is often better to reluctantly say "no" than to reluctantly say "yes".

d. That when a customer owes you, you make sure you collect your entitlement. Be nice about it, but be very firm and hardnosed. An easy face does not usually elicit settlement of debts

e. You never refuse any payment no matter how small the proportion, once a debtor customer elects part payment.

Cash Control in Practice

There are four major areas of concern in cash planning and control. These are:

a.   Incomes
b.   Expenditures
c.   Debtors
d.   Creditors

Before you can effectively control your cash position rather than your cash position controlling you, you must have a good grasp on all the items enumerated above.

Starting from the revised feasibility projections, we construct the year's sales and income budget. This is reduced to quarterly figures to cater for seasonal variations. It is then converted usually to monthly figures but occasionally to weekly forecasts.

The income forecasts are then reduced to cash basis so as to allow for credit sales and deferred payments.

For instance, if half your sales are likely to be cashed and the remaining half on credit basis, you need to go deeper to see within how many months you expect the debtors to pay in full. For instance, whilst most well established companies may be expected to settle their bill within two months, supply to government organization may take much longer. Thus, you will spread the year's estimated sales plus any opening debtor balances, into a chart containing the 12months of the year, after carefully working out how much cash will accrue in each month, from cash sales, credit sales and other income.

In like manner, a forecast of the likely expenditure both capital and recurrent will be made for the year per quarter and monthly. Under each month will be inserted the actual payment to be made in that month. If the cost of a capital purchase is to be settled in say two instalments for example, the cash payment will be inserted in the columns for the appropriate months.

Not all the recurrent expenses for one month may need to be made in cash in the month concerned. For example, salaries of employees may be subject to deductions for outstanding loans, so also may tax need be deducted for subsequent payment to those concerned.

Some purchases will have to be made in cash whilst some may be on credit which may extend to two months or even more. Each item of planned expenditure will have to be examined closely so as to determine when the incidence of cash disbursement will fall; provision must also be made for the settlement of debts brought forward from the previous month.

From the specific month's cash income duly totalled, is deducted the total cash expenditure for the month. If the income is higher, we have a cash surplus for the month, if the expenditure is higher; you have a cash deficit for the particular month. To this figure of surplus is added the surplus brought forward from the previous month to arrive at the surplus carried forward.

When the cash income is less than the cash expenditure, the difference is called a cash deficit. If the cash deficit is subtracted from the opening cash surplus and the deficit is still larger than the surplus, we have a net cash deficit carried forward which you need to control.

There are usually three ways out:
a.   You should try to increase the cash income
b.   You could endeavour to reduce or retime some cash expenditure and
c.   We have a cash resource gap which has to be bridged

This is usually done by arranging bank overdraft or loan.

Preparing your cash plan loan in advance will inform you of your resources gap long in advance so as to enable you approach the bank in very good time. A rushed and desperate application for bank assistance has more chances of failure than of success.

If the monthly resource gaps are of a fluctuating nature, that is surplus in one month and deficit in another or a deficit of about the same amount being carried forward, if it is not more than the value of one month or two months banking turnover, it can usually be bridged by overdraft facilities.

However, if the cash resource gap is forever widening, then you have an indication that a more serious problem exists and there may be need for recapitalization to inject more shareholders or seek longer term finance.

Where your cash plans reflect increasing cash surpluses, you should examine the possibility of short term deposits rather than leaving the balance idle in cash or current account where it can quite easily be looked.

Main Instrument of Cash Control

Documentation and record keeping are very crucial to effective cash planning and control. However, the documentation for a small enterprise need not be as comprehensive as those required to control the fortunes of a multi-million naira undertaking.

Whatever the system in practice, design of the control mechanisms must at the barest minimum entail.

a.   pre-expenditure planning
b.   pre-commitment authorization
c.   process of cash receipt and release and
d.   post-payment feedback.

Pre-expenditure Planning

There are two important parts of this which we had discussed earlier:
a.   the operating budget and plan operation
b.   the cash budget or cash forecast

Pre-commitment Authorization

Control is no longer possible once somebody who has ostensible authority has legally committed an enterprise. Once an order has been given, a purchase order has been delivered to the supplier or payment has changed hands, it is too late to exercise control.

In other to prevent embarrassment of each commitment, we can adopt a system of expenditure authorities. It is sometimes also called "proposed expenditure sensation".

Expenditure Authorities

Then first step is to determine the different levels of authority and the monetary value for which persons in each can commit the enterprise. The level may be as follow:
1.   The board of directors
2.   Executive committees of the board
3.   The chief executive
4.   Heads of departments and
5.   Manager of section

Depending on each enterprise and its key individuals, the

financial usually range from N10 at the grade of sectional manager to N100,000 or more for the level of the Chief Executive. The Board's levels are governed by the Memorandum Articles of Association.

It must be made clear that no one is allowed to split a large expenditure to smaller components. All proposed expenditure must be within the approved budget or plan and under the control of the authority officer, Mr. A cannot commit the budget under Mr. B

The system works as follow:

The person in charge of the budget would raise the expenditure authority, give it a Department Number and show the following particulars:

a.   Date
b.   Section or department
c.   The full detail of proposed expenditure
d.   The amount involves
e.   The budget item number
f.   Total value of the budget
g.   Amount committed to date
h.   Amount available in the budget
i.   Additional or background reference resolution etc
j.   Signature of the authorizing officer

it will then be sent to the finance (control) Department where it will be countersigned if the detail are in order or carried otherwise and returned to the sender. For higher amounts, it will be:

a.   Originated at the sectional level
b.   Signed by the head of Department
c.   Vetted by the finance section, and
d.   Approved or recommended by the Chief Executive and approve by the Chairman depending on the amount

it is only after the commitment has been authorized that the purchase order can be given to an external party to supply the service or product.

Official Receipts

Official receipts must be issued for all moneys received and duplicate copies retained normally for six years or more.

Process of Cash Release

All payment receipt must be documented that is to say; payment voucher must be raised, checked, passed and cross-checked and paid.

A payment voucher can either be a cheque-voucher or a cash-voucher. All vouchers must contain the following minimum details:

a.   Date
b.   Payee's name in full
c.   Payee's address in full (not merely box – number)
d.   Full detail of the transactions
e.   The supplier's invoice number
f.   The budget item number
g.   The pre-expenditure authority number

h.   A certificate that the goods or service have been duly supplied and used for official intended purpose.

Voucher checking

A payment voucher should be checked twice wherever possible. First by the section raising the payment voucher. second by an independent or internal audit section.

The second checking can either be prepayment or post payment. Both systems have considerable advantages as well as disadvantages which include economy, fraud prevention, corruption and bribery.

Finally, the person receiving the payment must always sign the payment voucher and if paid by cheque the receiver must sign as having received the cheque whose number must be quoted on the payment voucher. Paid payment voucher should be kept for 6 years or more.

Post Payment Feed-Back

Sequential and up to date records of all cash transactions must be kept.

It is very important to note that all accounting records should always be kept in a very strict order of date.

For a small scale enterprise, it may be advisable to keep a diary of all financial transactions on a daily basis and more economical to engage the services of an Account Clerk under the supervision of a consulting Book-Keeping Accounting Consulting Firm on a part-time basis

We need maintain a cash-book which may show in columnar form the following items for each expenditure.
1. Date
2. Detail
3. Reference
4. Amount
5. Capital
6. Material
7. Labour
8. Overhead

Under column 2, detail will be inserted the same of the payee of the payment voucher.

Under column 3, reference will be inserted then payment voucher number as well as the cheque number. The amount in the "Amount" column will also be extended to one of the four other columns as appropriate.

On the other side of the cash-book will be recorded all payment received by the enterprises under the following columns
1. Date

2.   Detail
3.   Reference
4.   Amount
5.   Sales
6.   Others

The column No 2 detail will consist of the name of the person paying the money.

Column No 3 reference will show the number of the official receipt issued to the payee. All other columns are self-explanatory.

It is important to emphasize that the two side of the cash-book must be totaled and balanced page by page

Those who may which to keep their accounting recorded by themselves may be well advised to devote about three weeks to reading books on book-keeping which may be found in many libraries.

For small enterprise it is possible to have an effective and simplified accounting forms and records system done for you by a professional firm of accountant or consultants. It is not advisable to endeavour to save money on accounting procedure, only to discover much later that innocent looking cashier or sales-clerk has swindled you of a lot of money. Most Nigerians will steal if allowed.

Cash Position Statement

This is usually provided weekly, but with enterprises having a sizeable amount of turnover and several bank accounts, it may be a daily affair.

It usually contains the following column on each page which is reserved for one bank account.
1.   Date
2.   Opening balance
3.   Lodgements
4.   Payments
5.   Closing balance
6.   Signature of chief executive

The cash position sheet is completed at the end of the day or week by transferring the total from the cash-book.

While allow the top official to see at a glance the summary of the appropriate cash position, without going through every detail of the cash-book, it serves as an effective alarm to slow down the speed of expenditure sections, or to improve the impart of revenue generation and collection.

Bank reconciliation Statement

the balance on the cash-book does not always agree with the balance show by bank statements. it is compulsory to identify all the reasons and the items as well as the amounts that make up difference through preparation of a bank reconciliation statement.

The item under each category should be arranged strictly in date order, starting from the oldest date to the most recent. The usual categories include:

a. Payment in cash book not yet made by the bank
b. Receipts in the cash book not yet cleared by the bank
c. Items of direct debtor i.e. bank charges not in cash book
d. Direct credit e.g. interest on deposit in bank statement but not yet in cash book

Each item should be resolve immediately. Those who cannot be resolved immediately should be reviewed with appropriate correspondence, through a special file called "Bank Reconciliation Statement and Correspondence".

CHAPTER TWO

PLANNING FOR SMALL BUSINESS

The topic implies that we have already chosen a particular business and we now have to plan for it. Put very simple, planning for a business involves combining the 3M's i.e. Man, Materials and Money, in such a way to achieve maximum operation results.

Let's take the resource we call MAN. The following points relates to him in our planning:

- Manpower requirements
- Organization chart
- Job specification
- Hiring
- Management

Manpower Requirements

For an entrepreneur to determine the manpower requirements, he must:

1. Be familiar with various steps of operation
2. Determine volume of work
3. Establish work Standard

Organization Chart:

This includes:

1.   Determining inter-relationship among various workers.

2.   Determining "who report to whom".

Job Specification

Tell each worker what he is supposed to do, assign responsibility and delegate authority.

Hiring

This has to do with the means of getting quality staff into your business.

Newspaper advertising is expensive but response is good

Labour office: Prospects of getting good response through this avenue is low. Job seekers use it as a last resort.

Hiring agency: The services of good agencies are expensive.

Although chances are good that they will select a good candidate, there is no guarantee that he will perform as expected on your particular job. Thus the hiring expenses may be a waste.

Institution placement centre: We can request that institutions send candidates to you. The services are free.

Present employees: Ask a good worker to help find a new employee: Chances are high that he will bring someone good.
Word of mouth: inexpensive, but could be slow to yield results.

Generally, a combination of methods is the best. If many positions are to be filled, newspaper advertisements are the most expedient. The National Youth Service Corp is another source of employees and it is free. Experience, in addition to basic training in relevant areas of interest, is vitally important. The candidate who has been exposed to procedures in other companies, can anticipate problems and solve them when they arise.

Experience has shown that it is rather difficult for small businesses to attract a high calibre dedicated workers, as they cannot offer the type of salaries and fringe benefits that the big companies offer. Apart from this, many workers are impatient for economic rewards and do not possess the foresightedness that the entrepreneur has regarding the business.

Management of People:
How do we get the most out of our workers and still keep them happy and satisfied with their jobs? Try the following

suggestions:

- ☐ Emphasize skills, not rules in your business.
- ☐ Set a high standard for your business.
- ☐ Know your subordinates and try to determine what is important to each
- ☐ Try to listen thoughtfully and objectively.
- ☐ Be considerate
- ☐ Be consistent
- ☐ Give your subordinates objectives and a sense of direction
- ☐ Give your directions in terms of suggestions or requests
- ☐ Delegate responsibility for details to subordinates
- ☐ Show your staff that you have faith in them and that you expect them to do their best.
- ☐ Keep your subordinates informed.
- ☐ let your subordinates in on your plans at an early stage.
- ☐ Allow subordinates a chance to take part in decisions.
- ☐ Tell the originator of an idea what action was taken and why.
- ☐ Try to let people carry out their own ideas.
- ☐ Build up subordinates' sense of value of their work.
- ☐ Let your people know where they stand.
- ☐ Criticize or reprove privately.

☐   Criticize or reprove constructively.

☐   Praise in public.

☐   Pass the credit on down to the operating people.

Effective communication is the key to successful management of people. Let me warn that lousy and lazy workers should be promptly terminated as soon as we notice that they are not amenable to change.

Materials: These are machines and other materials input like raw materials.

Poor quality materials may be cheaper to purchase, but they result in products of inferior quality. Supply of raw materials poses serious threats to business operations. Factors to consider include the followings:

Availability

Prices and price fluctuations

Delivery time

Mode of payment

Substitute raw materials.

Storage facility

Machines

Avoid religiously, any obsolete machine. If you can afford it buy new up-to- date machines instead of used ones; if you cannot, then settle for reconditioned ones. Buy two (2) small machines instead of one (1) large one; with the former option you can handle machines breakdown and slacks in production more efficiently.

Money

Financing a business is not an easy task. Under-financing is almost as bad as no financing at all, as it results in inefficiencies that can make it difficult for the business to make profit or even to recovers its investments. We should strive for more than enough money, so that we can take advantage of business opportunities.

Financial Planning and Management

Your ability to plan the financial needs of your new venture will play a big part in how much capital you will be able to raise. Prepare a loan package that includes your business plans, market analysis, projected balance sheet, profit and loss projections, and cash flow projections. Lenders prefer these financial projections is directly related to the amount of loan, how the loan money will be used, when the money will be needed, when the loan will be repaid, the source of repayment funds, and the amount of collateral you have to secure the loan. You should also include the amount of equity capital you are personally investing in the business venture.

Another part of the loan package should be personal

information about you and anyone else involve directly or indirectly in the new business. Don't assume the potential lender knows this information. Even if you have known each other for years, the leader may not have an accurate picture of your personal history and current financial situation.

The personal information included in the loan package should include education, work history and business experience of everyone involved in the new business. You should also include credit references, personal income tax statement for three years and updated financial statements. Information about the nature of the loan and personal histories of those involved may be a major factor in getting the loan. It is good you seek professional help with the financial projections and loan information. Your knowledge and understanding of the loan package will be important when the lender evaluates it.

The five Cs of credit

What do lenders look for in a loan package? You, the borrower, provide part of the information, but the potential lenders will also use their own credit files and outside sources. A traditional, time-tested checklist is the five Cs of credit: character, capacity, collateral, conditions and capital. By understanding each of these from the lender's viewpoint, you can anticipate your strong and weak points as they may appear to a potential leader.

1. **Character**

   To the potential lender, character means that you will make every possible effort to repay the loan. You must be a good manager, be honest, and have a good reputation as perceived by the lender. Therefore, it is important to be honest about your personal strengths and weaknesses.

2. **Capacity**

   Will your new business generate the cash flow to repay the loan? Do you have the capacity to repay loan? Lenders not only look at the business financial projections, but also your ability to repay the loan if the business does not work out as planned. Do you have outside income (investments, a working spouse)? Would you be able to return to your present job? Do you have other skills that could produce income? Be prepared to provide solid answers to these questions and be able to offer real evidence.

3. **Collateral**

   In case the new venture is not successful and the lender must foreclose, will the collateral cover the loan? Is the collateral marketable? In the past, a co-signer (someone who signs the loan along with you) has been used as collateral for many small business ventures. However, banks and traditional lending institutions now look less favourable at co-signer as collateral. Collecting from co-signers is becoming increasingly hard, and bankers then lose not one, but two customers. You can use your home or other real estates, cash value of life insurance policies or marketable securities as collateral for business loans. However, before borrowing against these items, consider carefully the consequences of the worst possible situation in your business if you are forced to liquidate.

4.   **Conditions**

Conditions are those factors over which you have little or no control. The lender will look at the conditions, or trends, in the overall business economy, the trend in your community, the seasonal character of your business, and the nature of your product or service. Other factors entering the decision-making process are whether the lender may have already invested in a competing business and how much competition there is in your market. Be prepared to tell the lenders how you plan to deal with these conditions, how you have assessed the market, and how your business will weather economic changes.

5.   **Capital**

Knowledgeable lenders will not put money into a new business unless they have concrete evidence that you have personally made a sizable financial commitment to the business. They know from experience that if the venture turns bad it will be easier for you to back out if you do not have your own money at risk. From your personal resources, you should try to provide as much of the needed capital as you can afford to put at risk. Depending on the capital needs, you cannot expect any lender to loan 80 percent or more of the capital, as they may for a home or investment real estate. New small businesses fail at a rapid rate and when they do fail, the assets cannot be easily turned into cash for payment of the loan. Therefore, a new business is a much higher risk for them than a home loan. You should expect to invest a much higher percentage of the needed capital for your new business.

Types of capital

Different types of small business requires different amounts and types of capital to get started. In some cases, the new business may only need capital for short period of time for inventory purchases or salaries. In other cases, facilities and equipment must be bought or leased, inventory purchased, and you must have enough cash left over to run the business until revenue can support the needed cash flow. Knowing the type and amounts of capital needed will help you figure out the best sources of capital for your new venture.

Equity versus debt capital

If you do not have enough personal capital, you can sell equity or you can incure debt. If shares of equity are sold in a partnership or corporation, the capital is not repaid, but the investor takes an ownership interest in the business and receives a portion of the business profits. Even though equity capital does not burden a new business with loan repayments and interest charges, it reduces the primary owner's shares of the profits. Debt must be repaid with interest, but normally the lender has no ownership control. Borrowing money at the very start of a new business will drain off income to make the debt payments.

Commercial loans

There are three types of commercial loans that are usually defined in terms of the length of time the loan is made.

Short-term commercial loans (30 to 90 days) are the most common loans made to a small business. They usually cover business operation expenses such as rent, insurance, advertising, inventory or salaries. Short-term loans are often unsecured and repayment is usually a lump sum, including interest when the loan matures.

Intermediate-term loans are for one to five years to purchase business equipment, buy fixed assets or provide working capital. Intermediate-term loans are usually secured by the new equipment or business assets. They sometimes have low monthly payments, with a large balloon payment at the end of the term.

A long-term commercial loan is for five years or more to purchase an existing business, buy real estate, or construct or improve a building or facility. The long-term loan is always secured by the assets for which the loan was made, usually requires constant monthly payments and often has a variable interest rate.

Ten Sources of Capital

With your new business plan, financial projections and financing knowledge, you are now ready to secure outside capital for your new venture. The following 10 types of financing sources are ranked according to amount of preparation required and ease of securing the outside capital. Less preparation to secure a loan does not mean it is the best source, nor the least expensive source of capital. Of course, there will be exceptions to these general statements about each financial source.

1. **Trade or supplier credit**

    Payment terms offered by your suppliers are potential sources of credit. Study the discounts for early payment and the penalty for late payment to determine the true cost of the credit. While some suppliers will extend credit only to well-established, proven firms, many will extend limited credit to new business to encourage another outlet for their merchandise. Planning for use of trade credit is essential. To establish good trade credit, a new business must make timely payment as agreed. Trade credit is effectively used by large businesses to buy products at lower cost than small firms. Do not depend too much on trade credit from one supplier. If repayment problems arise, you may find your major source for supplies cut off when you need it the most.

2. **Life insurance policies**

    A standard feature of most life insurance policies (except term insurance) is the owner's ability to borrow against the cash value of the policy. The money can be used for any business or personal need. It normally takes two years for a policy to accumulate sufficient cash value. You may borrow up to 95 percent of the cash value of the policy for an indefinite period of time. As long as you continue to pay the insurance premiums, the interest can frequently be deferred indefinitely. The policy loan will reduce the dollar value of policy and, in case of death, the loan is repaid first and then the beneficiaries receive the remainder. Some older life insurance policies guarantee very favourable rates.

3. **Friends and relatives**

It is best not to borrow from friends and relatives, but many people do. If you must borrow from a friend or relative, do it on a business basis by putting the agreement in writing. Check with a lawyer if you want a binding, legal agreement. You may also get a sample business loan contract form from a bank or lending institution. Use it as a basis for a written agreement that both parties find acceptable. Unrealistic and\ or naïve investment expectations have ruined many friendships and family relationships.

4. **Customers**

When customers pay for work in instalments as it is completed or provide some of the materials, they are, in effect, financing the business. For example, a carpenter reduces capital requirements when the customer purchases the building materials for a remodelling project. In addition, it is not uncommon to request a deposit from customers when ordering items, particularly special items.

5. **Leasing companies**

Leasing business equipment is another way to reduce capital needs. Everything from office furniture to food processing equipment can be obtained from leasing companies or commercial finance companies. Leasing is generally more expensive than bank financing and is limited to items that have a long serviceable life, widespread use, and are easily repossessed in the event of default. In many cases, you have the option to buy the equipment for an agreed upon amount at the end of the lease period.

6. **Commercial finance companies**

Commercial finance companies are generally seen as the place to go when you are unable to secure financing from a bank. Commercial finance companies, like banks, are concerned with your ability to repay the loan; however, they are more willing to rely on the quality of the collateral rather than your track record or profit projections. If you do not have substantial personal assets or collateral, a commercial finance company may not be the best place to secure start-up capital for a business. Commercial financing company capital is usually several percentage points higher than bank financing.

7.   **Commercial banks**

Commercial banks are by far the most visible lenders and make the greatest number and variety of loans. However, banks are generally conservative lenders. Although they accept collateral for business loans, loan approval rests on your ability to repay the loan as shown by your profit projections, management skills and your personal record. Strive to establish and keep a good working relationship with your banker. It may help to involve the banker in the planning process for your new business. Avoiding the banker until you need money may make a loan harder to get because the banker is unfamiliar with the business and its history.

8.   **Small Business Administration**

The Small Business Administration (SBA) is an independent government agency formed in 1953 to help small businesses in some advanced countries of the world. The SBA provides loan guarantees, participates with bank loans, and, if funds are available, makes a limited number of direct loans, to receive financial help from SBA, a business must be unable to secure reasonable financing from other sources. A business must also fit the SBA's generalized criteria for a small business, which varies for different types of business.

SBA loan interest rates vary from year to year based on the cost of money to the government. Also, the maturity of a SBA loan is limited to 10 years, except for the purchase or construction of building that may have a maturity of 20 years. A loan proposal for the SBA is generally more complex and more documented than one for banks. Unlike commercial lenders, the SBA will sometimes ignore a losing track record if a business shows signs of improvement with a healthy future. The activities of SBA are limited to some advanced countries of the world, not yet in Nigeria.

9.   **Small-business investment companies**

Small business investments companies (SBIC) are privately owned companies that are licensed and regulated by the SBA. SBICs were created to supply equity capital, long-term loan funds and management help to small-scale businesses. Most investment companies prefer to lend to established companies or finance purchases of existing businesses. In western world, the effects of SBIC is yet to be felt in Nigeria as is not in place yet.

10. **Rural economic and community development agency**

The rural economic and community development agency (RECDA) will guarantee term loans to non-farming businesses in rural areas. The guarantees can cover up to 90 percent of the total loan from a private lending institution, and there is no loan limit for one company. The RECDA requires the same extensive loan documentation as the SBA. However, RECDA's goal is to improve rural areas and, therefore, the agency requires more detail on number of jobs to be created and the impact the new business would have on overall employment in an area. Unfortunately, Nigeria is yet to have this type of agency, though there is industrial bank that gives loan to those businessmen or industrialists who meet the requirements.

11. **Philanthropist**

Some philanthropists give financial assistance to people to begin a business of their own.

12. **Religious houses**

Some large religious organizations also give financial assistance to unemployed to start a business of their own.

13.   Selling unused properties

Some valuables but unused can be sold by someone who is desperate to execute lucrative business plan. It may be an inherited property from one's parents that are not used. One should only do this when it is sure that the business is viable and profitable. Instead of keeping such properties without any benefit, it could be sold or used to raise money for one's business.

CHAPTER THREE

MANAGEMENT

Definition

Management is the act of getting things done through efficient and effective planning, organization, control and coordination of the activities of people.

Functions of manager

Regardless of their specific situations, all managers have the following functions in common:

1.   Planning
2.   Organizing
3.   Coordinating, and
4.   Controlling.

Let us discuss the functions beginning with the first.

Planning

All managers have a responsibility to plan. Planning entails deciding in advance what to do, how to do it, where to do it, and who is to do it. It involves setting the objectives of the enterprise and those of any departments within the organization.

Without clear-cut objective or goal, a business enterprise will get nowhere.   You need to set out the goals or objectives you want the enterprise to achieve.

For instance, you need to specify what kind of service or product you want to provide to society. You need to decide the amount of profit acceptable to you, and so on.

Apart from setting objectives, you need to decide how you are going to provide the services or product, who is to do what. You will also have to decide when the service or product is to be provided and where and what quantities and quality.

As you can see, planning involves hard thinking and decision-making. In many cases, you have to gather facts in order to make a good decision. For instance, if you are planning the location of your business, you need to collect information about possible, locations and evaluate the locations on the basis of their potentials, to enabling your business make enough sales to make an acceptable level of profit.

In general, planning ranges from planning daily tasks to making long-range projections. In other words, there are short-range plans and there are long-range plans. In all cases, your plans must be specific and clear enough to be communicated to all concerned.

Planning is very important in every aspect of life. Its importance in business is critical for success. Without a good plan and efficient and effective implementation of the plan, the business cannot succeed.

Good planning is a starting point for successful business management. If you want to be in business or you want to be a manager, planning is an essential skill you must acquire.

If you want to establish a business enterprise, you must learn to plan. A good feasibility study is one of the most important steps in starting a new enterprise. You cannot do without it because it constitutes your BUSINESS PLAN.

Planning is the most basic of all managerial functions. It is concerned with determining the objectives of the enterprise, the selection of departmental goals and the ways of achieving the objectives and goals.

Planning and control go together. No unplanned action can be controlled. The objective of control is to ensure performance according to plan or to prevent deviations from plans. Plans thus serve as standards for control. He who fails to plan, plans to fail.

Organizing

A manger's organizing function involves identifying the jobs to be done and organizing them so that they can be done efficiently. Specific organizing tasks include the following: grouping jobs in meaningful relationship, selecting members of workgroups, delegating authority, and establishing a network of interaction that will lead to the achievement of the organization's objectives.

Another aspect of organizing function that is very important is staffing. This involves specifying the skills or abilities needed, evaluation and selecting applicants, making plans for their remunerations or compensation and their organizational goals and those of the employees.

Steps in Organizing

The following are the steps:

1. Establishment of objectives.
2. Formulation of supportive objectives, policies and plans.
3. Identification and classification of activities necessary to accomplish these.
4. Grouping the activities in the light of human and material resources available and the best way of using them.
5. Delegating to the head of each group the authority necessary to perform the activities, and

6. Trying these grouping together horizontally and vertically, through authority relationships and information systems.

Coordinating

Another key management function is coordinating. The aim of coordinating is to synchronize and harmonize the activities of departments of an organization in order to achieve the common organizational goals. In other words, it aims at making sure that all departments or members of the organization are working towards the achievement of the common goal of the organization. Coordination demands high level leadership qualities on the part of the chief executive of the firm.

The organization structure (i.e. how the firm is organized) has an influence on coordination, because the organization determines the frame work that governs all lines of command, channels of communication, and patterns of relationships that must be harmonized by the chief executive.

Coordinating Techniques

The following are the coordinating techniques that managers apply to ensure harmony and integration of the organizational effort towards the achievement of the organizational goal:

1.   Consultative management

2.   Conference

3.   Communication.

The above techniques should be self-explanatory. Consultation management entails promoting cooperative effort and making use of the "group mind". This is similar to the master-mind principle discussed in Ifechukwu's book: The Science of Wealth. When a manager applies the consultation management techniques he seeks the assistance, opinion and expertise of his subordinates in solving management problems. Nobody in this world has all the answers to all problems.

Seek advice, help and cooperation of your subordinates in solving management problems. This is what management is all about, getting things done through people.

Controlling

The last major management function we shall discuss is controlling. Controlling is concerned with measurement and correction of the performance of the activities of subordinates in order to ensure that enterprise goals and plans are being achieved. This is a function every manger must perform irrespective of his rank or position in the organization.

Pre-requisites of Control Systems

Two conditions must be met before you can devise or maintain a system of control. These conditions are:

1. Control must be based on plans. The plans must be clear and integrated. Unless there is a plan of action, it is difficult to determine what to control. Plans become the standards by which achievement or deviations from plans are measured.

2. Control requires organization structure. Since the purpose of the control function is to measure the activities and take necessary action to ensure that plans are being achieved, you must know where in the enterprise the responsibility for deviating from plans and taking action to make correction lies.

Steps in the Control Process

The basic process involves the following steps:

1. Establishing standards
2. Measuring performance against standards
3. Correcting deviations from standards and plans.

Establishing Standards

Standards are of many kinds. They may be stated in quantitative or qualitative terms. That is to say, we may state them in quantitative terms or merely describe them in terms of quality. Among the best standards are goals which are verifiable.

Since the end result for which people are responsible are the best measures of achievement, they furnish excellent standards of control.

Standards, as earlier pointed out, can be stated in physical or quantitative terms such as quantities of products, unit of service, labour-hours, speed, or they may be expressed in monetary terms such as volume of sales, costs, capital expenditures, or profits.

Let us give an example. Suppose, you want to set standards or goals for your sales department. This you can set after due consultation with the manager concerned to ensure that the standards are not only realistic but also to engender cooperation of the people who will be expected to carry out the plans.

Thus, you may specify a definite volume or level of sales to be attained by the sales department. This expected sales volume or level becomes the standard by which you can measure the performance of the sales department. If the department performs below the standard, you have to find out why and take corrective action.

Similarly, for example, you can set standards in terms of

quantities of products or man hours to be achieved by those working for you. You then use the standards as a basis for measuring their performance thereby performing your control function.

With our discussion of the control function we come to the end of our discussion of the basic functions of management. As a manger you must be able to perform the four basis function in order to manage your business or department as the case may be successfully.

CHAPTER FOUR: HOW TO APPLY AND GET BANK LOAN

Introduction- The Ify millionnaire

The street is full of Ify millionaires and thousandnaires. Almost everyone you meet, morning, noon and evening, has one "sure banker" idea or another which can make him or her, a very wealthy and comfortable entrepreneur, an instant millionaire, that is, if only the highest and sometimes the only from culture between the people (of which you are likely one) and the millions and thousands is finance- project finance, risk finance. "If I can get money" "if someone would help me" etc. etc! thus anyone who can agree to give you a single kobo so that you can do business, is giving you considerable help, and lifting you away from the millions of "Ify millionaires" to a real and successful one, that person can be yourself, your parent, your wife or husband, your friend, your parent-in-law, or an acquaintance, long or chance, or as a matter of last resort, a bank or finance institution.

What banks are not and why – a question and answer series

S/N	Question	Your Answer
1	Why should a bank manager give you money which neither your friends, your parents or in-laws will give or trust you	

	with?	
2	How can the bank manager trust you more than those who have known you for years?	
3	Especially, why should a bank manager loan you money which somebody else has entrusted to his care for the safety custody?	
4	Do you know the owner can come for it at any time, most often without notice?	
5	If you are a bank manager, will you lend such entrusted money generously or reluctantly?	
6	To a familiar person or a total stranger?	
7	Familiar in what way?	
8	To someone who you can trust, or whose character you cannot vouch for?	
9	Will you ensure the borrower does not escape with the money?	
10	If so, how will you do it?	
11	Will you be very stringent or not about guarantee or security?	

12	Even if there is guarantee, will the person who put his money in your safe custody be satisfied with taking the guarantee, in replacement of his money if the "tycoon" does not repay?	
13	What steps, can you take, to ensure that you will not be left with an embarrassing guarantee, at the end of the day?	
14	Will you, in fact, ask questions, to ensure that the proposed project is not a foolish gamble?	
15	What question will you ask?	
16	What answers will satisfy you? Vague assurance, dubious hopes, conservative assumptions or flamboyant guesse?	
17	Your questions and answers, will they be oral chitchat, or in clear black and white?	
18	Will you say "yes", to all applicants to use the safe keepers money, or to only very few?	
19	Will the conditions need to be	

	fulfilled before, whilst taking, or after taking the loan?	
20	Even for those you say "yes" will you lay down conditions?	
21	Which is the primary duty of banks, to safe keep your money, or to sponsor tycoons?	
22	If so, what conditions?	
23	Of two applicants, 'A' has got 80% of the money he needs, while B has next to nothing which of the two will you rather support A or B?	
24	Why will you not support the other?	
25	Of two applicants, A willing and able to repay the loan in say two or three years, and B asking to repay in six, or seven years, which will you prefer to help? WHY?	
26	Once the loan is paid out, will you forget the whole business until the safe depositor comes for it, or will you indeed keep an eye on the borrower, how the loan is	

	being used how the business is and how the loan is being repaid?	
27	If so, how can you be able to do this? BY little informal chance-talks, or in written formalized reports?	
28	Will you be satisfied with paper reports alone, or will you sometimes go and see things for yourself	
29	If customers A and B took loans from your bank, A paid back as promised, C did not, which of the two will you help again with customer's safekeeping money?	
30	And which experience will guide you more in future?	
31	Of your experience with Mr. A who repaid in full, or with Mr. C who failed you, with which one, will you pre-judge most applicants in future until convinced otherwise?	
32	Then for what minimum period will you have "known" a	

	customer through his or her account before you can consider his or her application to borrow other peoples' deposits?	
33	Most banks demand 6 months minimum familiarity, is this too short, too long, or adequate?	
34	**Credibility and Authenticity** Of two customers, Mr. A and B, the proposals and calculations of A were prepared by "LOP' a well known firm of reliable consultants, while Mr. B's were done by some unknown expert", or by himself, which of two reports will you be inclined to believe and support with the money kept in your safe custody?	
35	**Age of Viability Projections** Suppose as a bank loan officer, you received two reports containing the calculations and the assumptions on which the possibility that each loan can be repaid are based, one report is	

	twelve months or more old, and the other was prepared about 6 weeks before, which one will you rely on?	
36	What considerations will tend to inform or guide your tendency?	
37	Can a market change materially in say 4 or 6 months?	
38	How old will you think a viability report should be at the most?	
39	If too old, what advice will you give the applicant?	
40	**Timing of Application** Suppose applicant A gave you his application and proposals one week before the project is to start, and applicant B gave you his own three months before the anticipated start off, which of the two applications is more likely to succeed?	
41	Why should that be the case?	

You should always involve and interest your bank manager in your project as early as you can, and if possible, right from its inception and planning stage. Do not wait until your financial situation has gotten desperate, or your project stalemated and stranded, before rushing to the bank for help.

An economics of bank loans

As you know the moneys which depositors save with banks can earn some interest for the owners. This is about 10% per annum or as decided by the central bank generally. Also when a bank manager lends you the money, he charges interest now generally 15% p.a. This 15% works out at 1.23k per naira per month, as against a charge of 10k per naira per month charged by private money lenders. Thus while a loan of ₦10,000 will cost you ₦125 per month from a bank, the same loan will cost you ₦1000 per month if obtained from a money lender. What interest rate is this? Work this out.

You can see why so many people rush for bank loans.

An Economics of Bank Loan Failure

For the ten thousand naira (#10,000 loan) granted to you, the bank's gross margin is 5% when the bank manager has paid the depositor a minimum of 10% and received interest of 15% from you. Sometimes the bank may have to pay the depositor as much as 14% leaving only a margin of 1%

from which the bank must pay its rents, staff salaries, staff allowances, and all other running costs before declaring a profit.

Suppose the margin is not 1% but say 2% then on the ₦10,000 loan granted to you, the manager makes a profit of ₦200 only. Suppose the loan was granted to Mr. X who lavished it, or mismanaged his business, and cannot repay, the ₦10,000 is lost. How much new loan must the bank manager give in order to make a compensating income totalling ₦10,000? Work it out yourself.

Since ₦200 was earned from a loan of ₦10,000, how much loan will earn ₦10,000?

Another loan of ₦10,000 or new loan of ₦500,000?

Suppose the new loan of ₦500,000 goes bad, how much loan will the bank have to give in order to recover both the first ₦10,000 and the second ₦500,000?

We can then clearly begin to see and appreciate why banks and their managers have to be very cautious, and stringent, when considering applications for loans.

You can also now begin to understand not only how, but also when, to apply for and get a bank loan. Once we are able to provide reasonable answers to all the key questions, we are almost through our course on how to apply for and get bank loans.

Two types of bank loan facilities

When we talk of bank loans we may be talking either about a loan proper or an overdraft facility. Because the appropriateness and efficient usage of both types of facility differ, and because the criteria for judging an application for an overdraft facility have some important additional differences from those applicable to a loan, it is important to know when to apply for one or the other, so as to enhance the chance of success.

An application that may succeed if called and assessed as a loan application may fail if called or evaluated as an application for an overdraft facility.

Whilst a loan is given in bulk and has to be repaid usually in instalments which may be monthly, quarterly or yearly and therefore reduces specifically until fully liquidated, an overdraft is used up gradually, and tends to be permanent in nature, prone to increase rather than reduce, and is renewable yearly until it is "recalled": a term which means a request to repay the full amount and put the overdrawn account back into balance.

A loan is credited to your bank account as if you made a lodgement. An overdraft facility permits you to draw cheque beyond the balance to your credit but subject to the limit of the overdraft. When you draw a cheque, your overdraft is increased, when you lodge in your sales proceed, your overdraft is reduced.

Interest is chargeable on both a loan account and an overdraft account. Whereas the main test of how much loan you can get is how realistically your records show you can safely repay the loan instalments as and when due, your application for an overdraft is greatly affected by the level of your monthly turnover.

It is important to know that whilst the level of your loan may be so high than that which your monthly credit balance or surplus can repay with interest, the level of your overdraft should not normally exceed your total turnover of two months, that is to say the bank will usually approve your overdraft if the amount is such that your operations' Previous performance over the past six months, show that your monthly turnover equals half the level of overdraft being applied for.

Perhaps we need to emphasize very strongly that the turnover will be calculated only by reference to the lodgements made into your bank account during the period. Thus the larger the total value of the lodgements even if being always withdrawn, the higher the overdraft you can have. The cash you receive and spend for purchases without going through your bank account reduces your turnover, and therefore severely limits your capability to enjoy overdraft facilities.

Thus if your average monthly sale lodged into your account over six months amount to ₦10,000, you can safely apply for overdraft of ₦20,000. If at the end of twelve months when the facility is due for renewal your monthly sales have risen to say N25,000, the facility will most likely be renewed, and could be raised from N20,000 to a maximum of N50,000 that is ₦25,000x 2= ₦50,000.

On the other hand, if because you were receiving cash from customers and making purchases in cash without making lodgements and withdrawals, so that even if your average monthly sales total ₦25,000 or more, but you had only been banking the net margin (cash sales ₦ 25,000 minus cash purchases ₦20,000) of say ₦5,000 monthly, your overdraft may still be renewed, but the amount will be cut from ₦20,000 to ₦10,000 (i.e. 2 x ₦5,000). This means you will have to find immediately, ₦10,000 cash with which to reduce your debt, or in banking parlance "regularize the position" the importance of lodging every naira of your sales into your account and withdrawing it even on the same date is to pay for purchases, cannot therefore be too strongly emphasized.

When to use which facility

Circumstances differ in which loans and overdrafts are appropriate. As a general rule, an overdraft should be used to defray costs which directly and continuously add to turnover or value added. These include stocks, wages and operating overheads such as electric and telephone bills.

Where the intention is to finance assets or other long term, one-time, expenditure, such as reconditioning of a broken down machine, or paying rents in advance for use over many months or years, the more appropriate finance will be a loan, which may be repaid instalmentally, over the useful life of the assets, or during the term of its contribution to your operation or less. This is because the purchase of a big machine or building cannot immediately affect your turnover as will say the purchase of resale stocks or the wages of your staff.

Therefore in submitting your application to a bank for financial assistance, you should Endeavour to separate one time, long term, asset expenditures, from short-term finance of operational day-to-day activities. Whilst the latter should be financed by overdraft facilities, the former should be by way of a loan repayable over an agreed term.

Necessary distinction should be made in your application to

this effect. Whilst you can usually get a loan beyond the limit of several months' turnover, you may not get overdraft beyond two months average turnover in the six months last preceding the date of evaluation.

When trouble comes

Sooner or later you are bound to hit financial trouble. Some trusted supplier or customer may betray you. Employees may cause you severe losses, or the market for your product may alter so severely as to disrupt and weaken your financial position and ultimately paralyze your operations. You may end up with hardly any employee at all but a huge and embarrassing bank debt. Almost every successful businessman or woman that you may know has gone through this experience at least once before, some, more than once. Right now, very many Nigerians are going through baptism of fire.

It is in times like this that you will find that the bank manager or loan officer who was always pleased to see you and gladly attended your child's naming ceremony. Or sent you greeting cards, has suddenly turned very sullen and stern. You should not lose heart. You should not run away from the bank.

In this situation, it is possible that when you lodge money

in, you may not be allowed to draw. You will then begin to agree that a banker is a friend who gives you an umbrella when the sky is a stone dry only to withdraw it at the slightest sniff of a down pour. In that circumstance, most Nigerians tend to move to another bank and open a new account. That is a great error.

Banks hate being abandoned. Bankers abhor anyone who tries to look too smart for them or makes them feel cheated or fooled. When you are no longer operating your account, it is term "dormant" and a dormant overdrawn account is one thing which bank managers never pray to meet or tolerate in the course of transactions.

Whether it is true or not, the bank manager knows you are not living on air and tap-water alone. He knows you are spending money on daily maintenance, and the money must be coming from somewhere, being drawn from somewhere when needed, and therefore being probably kept with a rival bank. There is therefore no offence as grievous to the bankers as a customer abandoning an unpaid loan or overdraft account. Banks, will go to almost any length to pursue such customers, and forcefully but legally, recover such indebtedness. Never jilt your bank.

Seeing that "no condition is permanent", Nigerians bankers are, more than elsewhere, willing to give a debtor a second, third and even fourth chance. The crucial thing is to keep your bank manager in the full picture of your circumstances, and the genuine efforts you are making, to keep the account going.

The last thing you should ever do therefore when trouble knock through your bank account is to run. Rather, you should stay undaunted and maintain the account at all cost. There are many ways of achieving this, but whatever your tactics always give prompt and sensible reassuring replies to each letter you receive from the bank.

If your loan was to be repaid at say ₦500 per month and you can now make only ₦500 per month gross, rather than pocket all, if you are forthright with your bank manager, you may be allowed to lodge all, and draw anything from 50% to 80% of your lodgements. You can usually renegotiate your repayment terms. This is called "restructuring".

Under it, your overdraft of say ₦100,000 may be repackaged into say an overdraft of ₦10,000 and a loan of ₦90,000 which loan may now be spread and repayable over 3 to 5 years, instead of immediately. Also a term loan with say 24 monthly instalments may be rescheduled:

a.	To give a repayment moratorium (during which no instalment payment is made) of say 6 months, and

b.	To extend or elapse the agreed repayment period to

say 36 months inclusive or exclusive of the agreed moratorium.

Whatever you do, the greatest danger is to ignore "recall" or "pressure" letters on your account. You should always Endeavour to go and talk to the manager first and follow up with a reasonable reassuring reply thereafter.

If you are able to weather the storm under the revised easier terms, it is all the more to your benefit as the bank will appreciate your loyalty and integrity and should the occasion ever arise (as they often do) they will be willing to assist you once again. It is certainly true to say that the longer the duration and the higher the aggregate value of your transactions with a bank, the larger the value of other people's money which the managers will be willing to lend to you, that is what is called confidence, it is a function of both length of time and size of transactions, not just one, or the other, but both.

Summary

You should establish clearly and realistically what business you want to venture into. You should provide, if possible a major part of the finance required through your own resources or those of relation, and seek a bank's help only for the smaller balance. As generous as banks can be, they are not likely to finance more the 2/3 of your total cost.

CHAPTER FIVE

RAW MATERIAL SOURCING IN NIGERIA

In this chapter, attempt will be made to define what raw materials are and how they can be sourced locally. A list of small scale industrial groups will be drawn based on their raw materials needs' and their potential sources. He will discuss to some extent technologies involved in the raw materials production and will consider the problems that small scale industrialists may encounter in sourcing their raw materials locally. Also, we will attempt to outline areas which we think the government can readily be of help.

What are raw materials and why source them locally?

Raw materials can be aptly described as those materials which are transformed (by some means) from their obtainable forms into finished products which are suitable for use by the end users or sometimes into intermediate products which may need to be further processed. They could be starting materials or added during the course of production, but it is certain that nothing can be produced without them.

The major reason for sourcing for raw materials locally is the economic independence it grants local production and particularly for small scale industries the facilitation of continuous production.

It must be noted that small scale industries are either producing raw materials for industries e.g. those producing starch for further conversion into pharmaceutical bidders etc. or using existing raw materials e.g. iron mongers into utilize metals for making gates, etc.

In sourcing these materials however, a number of factors must be considered and this includes availability, abundance, purity and cost.

Availability

The industrialist must first ensure that the raw materials for his production is available or can be available. Non-living resources vis-à-vis living resources.

Abundance

This is based on the extent or potential of the raw materials. Once it is established that these materials are available, and then the relative abundance should be determined. The need for the material may need to be projected to estimate how long it may last the industry taking into consideration competing industries.

Purity and cost

After its relative abundance is established, the state and purity in which it occurs would determine the cost at which it will be obtained. There may be other factors such as social factors which may need to be examined.

Classification of industries and their raw material needs

Under this section, we have classified various industries based on their raw material needs and the problems that may face them in getting their requirements. The groups are as follows:

1. Processed cereal based industries
2. Edible oil and fat
3. Petrochemical based industries
4. Inorganic material based industries
5. Metal product and wood products
6. Animal products
7. Food products and others

Processed cereal based industries

The industries in this group include bakery, brewing, beverages etc. the major raw materials are cereal, e.g. maize, millet, sorghum, wheat. There is abundant supply of cereals in the country.

Edible oil and fats

The industries in this group include vegetable oil production, soaps and detergents, margarine etc. the raw material is vegetable oil which is obtained from oil bearing seeds such as melon, soya beans, oil palm, coconut, sunflower, cotton seed etc.

The by-product of this group is residual cake which may be further processed into livestock feeds. These oil bearing seeds grow well in Nigeria and abound all year round.

Petrochemical based industries

This group includes plastics, polymers etc. the products are petroleum based and presently, Nigeria produces quite a number of petroleum products from its several refineries.

Inorganic material

Under this category are the cement industries, chalk and other chemicals. There are several inorganic materials deposits in the country but the mining of these materials require a high capital outlay.

Metal products

These include products such as nails, wire nettings, furniture frames etc. presently, Nigeria has a rolling mill in operation, and effort are on to commission other iron-based projects. The aluminium industry is also gradually picking up. Wood is mainly used for construction purposes and for making furniture etc. The wood is obtained from trees which are fell in the forests. Thus they abound in the forest region of the country.

Animal products

Under this category are the fisheries, livestock and wild life. The major use into which they are part is feeding human beings. They may be classified into flesh foods such as fish and meat and non-flesh products such as eggs, leather etc. Nigeria is blessed with a good resource base, but efforts should be made to sustain the growth of this resources thus, area which industrialists can readily invest are, fish farming, and animal farming.

Food products

There are various categories of food products such as roll crop based foods, vegetables and fruits. This area has been neglected for some time but unfortunately we have realize this and efforts are being made to revamp the resources based of this country.

From the classification done above, it is obvious that there is one area which is most important and that is agriculture. This is because agriculturally based raw materials would be the most likely source of raw materials for the small scale industries. The other areas e.g. petrochemical would require large capital investments that the small scale industrialist cannot afford.

Problems of small scale industrialists in sourcing raw materials locally

1. Lack of information on the abundance/potentials of properties of resources and commodities.
    Solution: Databank, government extension, training to reflect local content demonstration.
2. Poor market information system for identifying potential markets for raw materials.
    Solution: Better system of information dissemination by government, small scale investors to conduct their own survey and gradually improve on it with time.
3. Imported technology and equipment
    Solution: Adopt locally developed or adapted appropriate technology.
4. Poor project design
    Solution: Consult experienced organizations and individuals.
5. Poor quality of raw materials (adulteration, poor production steps, packaging, quality control, storage etc.)
    Solution: Improved output must result from deliberate effort to improve quality raw materials, process and final product control, scheduling of production etc.
6. Lack of storage facilities for perishable and non-perishable materials.
    Solution: Provision of such facilities by government and relevant agencies at affordable prices.
7. Continuous production
    Solution: Proper scheduling of raw materials

purchase and use

CHAPTER SIX

EVALUATING A BUSINESS PROPOSAL

The emphasis of this chapter is on the evaluation of a business proposal from a financier's point of view. The financier in this case will be limited to a banker or a potential investor (whether an individual or a company). The one thing all financiers have in common is that they all ask the question 'is the business worth the risk?'

What is risk? Risk from a business point of view is simply the classification of the degree of probability of an error of judgment resulting in a loss of investment. There are several risks, both quantifiable which shall be discussed in a later section of this presentation. The analysis of a proposal generally falls into two categories, these are Quantifiable and Qualitative

It is assumed that the business proposal is presented by a limited liability company. The quantitative analysis as the name suggests has to do with "quantities" analysis of projections and other financial information. Qualitative analysis is otherwise known as 'number crunching'. The qualitative analysis on the other hand, has to do with other factors relevant to the success of the project but not denoted in numbers. In evaluating a business proposal, several key questions need to be asked under those broad outlines. Of prime importance are:

1.   The benefit to the banker/investor
2.   What is the proposal/project about? How much is required?
3.   Who are the sponsors? What is their contribution?
4.   What is the experience of the management team? This is particularly critical in project financing.
5.   What are the risks inherited in the proposal/project?
6.   Will the cash flows support the repayment schedule?
7.   What kind of security is being offered? Is it adequate to cover the perceived risks?

It is also important to bear in mind that some proposals while not attractive in the form in which they have been presented, may be restructured to better reflect both the applicants' needs and the requirements of the financier. This is often true in project finance.

1.   Benefit to the bank/investor
The benefits to the banker are in
i.   Fees
ii.   Spread income (the difference between the cost of funds and the lending rate)
iii.   Ancillary business in the form of export transactions, letters of credit lead managing syndications for the company, providing services for other affiliated companies.

The benefits to investors are usually in the form of:
i.   Dividends

ii.   Interest payments (for example, for debenture issue.)
iii.   Part ownership in the business with a share in the potential profits

2.   **What is the proposal about?**
        This involves a discussion of details of the project such as:
i.   Purpose of the required financing
ii.   Amount required, terms.

        If the proposal involves the establishment of an agricultural or manufacturing concern (project finance) other issues raised include:
i.   Product
ii.   Project capacity
iii.   Production techniques and other technical specifications included in a project cost breakdown
iv.   Financing structure detailing expected sources of financing equity, loans.

3.   **Who are the sponsors of the project? What company has sent the proposal?**
        The question seeks to establish the reputable of the sponsors
i.   Who is backing the project?
ii.   Whether they have been involved in projects of this nature
iii.   What their success rate is
iv.   How influential they are in terms of being able to influence in a positive way the success of the project (marketing the products, raising the required financing).

If the business/company which requires the loan is already

in existence wishing to expand, diversity or just seeking an overdraft facility for working capital needs, then there is already a financial history which indicates the strength/weakness of the company. The contribution of the sponsors is given under financing structure. A comparison of the total liabilities with the sponsor's contribution (otherwise known as equity) gives a ratio known as leverage. Leverage is an indicator of the level of acceptable debt a company can carry on its books. Acceptable debt levels vary depending on the sector/industry the project falls into. High leverages are usually acceptable for capital intensive projects/industries.

Management/financing history

The financial history of a company is often a good indicator of the capabilities of its management team. Financial analysis is the core of the quantitative analysis of a proposal/project. It involves:

i.   Ratio analysis which shows the financial strength of the company in terms of liquidity (current ratio/quick ratio) profitability (return on investment, return on assets) leverage (debt/equity) cost effectiveness etc.

ii.   Sensitivity analysis which subjects the projections of the company's future performance to changes in factors which could affect this performance. For example, what would happen if projected income is not realized because of a percentage drop in demand? How would it affect profit margins and the company's ability to repay its debts from cash flow?

Other indicators of management ability include company policies and strategies especially in relation to increasing market share by expansion, product diversification, backward integration etc.

Risks

There are several risks in many business proposals, some of which can be hedged against. The true test of good management is in the effective management of these risks. Similarly, the true of a good banker/investor is in the effective hedging against risks (barring the risk of a force majeure- a force majeure being such events as earthquakes, floods etc.). Risk fall into several categories viz:

(a)   **Political risk:** this is the risk of the business being affected by changes in government policies and strategies. Examples are the introduction of Second Tier Security Market (STSM), the ban on wheat, increase in tariffs for cotton and yarn which affect the textile industry. The only way to hedge the risk is to follow economic trends which may dictate changes in policy and to keep trends in 'high places'. Some political risks in developing countries like Nigeria cannot be hedged e.g. change in political power by coups and the attendants changes in government emphasis. This is the main reason why government-owned companies/parastatals are at such high risks – Board and Management can be changed at the drop of a hat.

(b) **Business risk:** this is the broad risk under which other risks have been classified.

i. **Market risk**: Will the product being promoted in the proposal find market acceptability? Can this acceptability be sustained? In effect can a permanent niche be created in the market? If the proposal is for the expansion of an existing line, is there sufficient demand for the product to justify the expansion?

ii. **Raw material risk**: Are the raw materials for production readily available? At what cost? The questions are particularly significant in the Nigeria of today where long term dependence on imported raw materials has rendered several industries vulnerable.

iii. **Foreign exchange rate**: How much foreign exchange is required for the successful completion of the project (if any)? With the limitations on the amount of foreign exchange available under STSM, how does the company purpose to satisfy its foreign exchange requirements?

iv. **Completion risk**: This is applicable mostly to start up projects. What factors could make the risk of completion higher than usual- what is the possibility of cost over-runs? Who will finance them? Is there a performance bond to ensure that the contractors complete the work according to the terms of the contract?

Will the cash flow support the repayment schedule?

This is the million dollar questions on which the ultimate

decision to lend or not to lend rests. For an investor, the question would be what is the potential profit level that would guarantee sufficient returns on any investment? An evaluation of all the assumptions used in the proposal for the income and cash flow projections is essential. In addition, sensitivity analysis needed to be carried out to test the validity of the assumptions.

Security and its adequacy

The most acceptable form of security in Nigeria are fixed assets higher in value than the financing required. This is because fixed assets hardly ever realize their full book value in a sale situation. Current assets are also attractive in addition to fixed assets. For reputable companies, negative pledges may be requested. Should the total assets of the company be considered insufficient guarantees, domiciliation of income (operating or other income such as rents receivable etc.) or the assets of the key shareholder (owners) may be requested. The security sought by banks is considered a secondary source of repayment in the event of a default. For the investor, there is no such security. All he holds is a share certificate which may or may not be worthless.

Very often, easiest business proposal to consider are those involving the provision of overdraft facility only. Overdraft are current line/short term facilities required for the normal operation of the business/company e.g. purchase of raw materials, financing of receivables, letter of credit activities, payment of salaries etc.

Sources of payment are usually normal cash flow from the operation of the business. The justification for the provision of the facility is therefore that in the short term. Cash flow derives from the business will be used to reduce the outstanding on the facility.

In spite of the extensive analysis carried out in the evaluation of business proposals especially by banks, it needs to be stated here, that there is no substitute for 'gut felling' all the figures may look right, but the project fells wrong. Listen to your instincts and take whatever precautions are called for in the form of more extensive analysis and additional security or don't do it.

CHAPTER SEVEN

DEVELOPMENT OF EXPORT-ORIENTED SMALL-SCALE INDUSTRIES IN NIGERIA

What is an export-oriented industry?

In the context of the export (incentives and miscellaneous provisions) decree no. 18 of 1986, any industrial enterprise which exports least 50% of its annual production can be regarded under this export legislation to be export-oriented. In addition, the product of such an industry must have 35% value added or 40% local material contents (the minimum original criteria under the ECOWAS trade protocol). Opinions do vary from country to country on the definition of an export-oriented industry. The proportion of the annual production of such an industry, being exported may vary from 10% to 100%. The 50% level set in Nigeria is in relation to precise export incentives or special advantages in form of tax reliefs or even total exemption being offered to such enterprises under the export legislation referred to above.

Sales to export markets will often fill in the seasonal "troughs" in demand so that factories can be kept busy all the year round and cash flow problems can be ceased.

Exporters have easy access to the foreign exchange they

generate and they can therefore import machinery and technology to improve their business.

From a personal point of view, it is more challenging, more interesting and more enjoyable to travel and work in international business environment than to be stuck in the narrow and unstimulating activities of a well-known home market.

Small scale industries as export-oriented base

Several developing countries have successfully developed and used medium to small-scale industries as a take-off base for their export promotion drive. India, Philippines and Taiwan are the leading examples of such countries.

The characteristics and the nature of organization of this category of industries have constituted the main source of success as a basis for the prosecution of an export promotion drive. In view of the fact that small-scale industries make the following contribution to the process of industrialization, namely:

(i.)   Value added generation;

(ii.)   Establishing links between agriculture and industry and utilizing local raw materials and waste products available in relatively small quantities;

(iii.)   Enhancing flexibility production and rapid market responses;

(iv.)   Using and harnessing existing traditional techniques of production, producing unique products, and (v.)   Labour intensive technology and low capital outlay.

Value added generation

Small-scale industries are usually industries which rely on local sources raw materials. Often they are 80% local raw material based. To this end, they fit in very well into the foremost economic criterion for export development and promotion i.e. having a comparative advantage in the production of an exportable product.

Small-scale agro-allied industries

This group of small-scale industries has the highest potentials for export development. Nigeria is endowed with rich natural resources ranging from food to fiber and forestry products. The waste products from large-scale industries already established in this sub-sector can constitute a good source of raw materials for export-oriented industries. For example, wood processing industries and furniture components manufacture. The sawdust wood industries are currently being exported whereas it could be processed further into particles for export for better value.

Flexibility of production and rapid market resources

One major advantage small-scale industries have over large scale industries is the nature of the technology employed and the simplicity as well as the flexibility in the method of production. Thus, SSIs are easily adaptable and can therefore rapidly respond to changing market demands. Small-scale manufacturers are better placed to take advantage of export opportunities in terms of demand for new product and the appearance of a new market.

The control and management of such industries are concentrated in an individual (the owner/manager), quick decisions are taken to meet with the challenging market situation. These characteristics of SSIs give them a great edge over the large-scale industries, which often slow in taking up the challenge of developing new product for export. The experience in Nigeria today has more than confirm this point, because the multinationals i.e. the UAC, John Holt, SCOA were initially reluctant to embrace the export promotion drive.

CHAPTER EIGHT

LEGAL REGULATORY FRAMEWORK FOR SETTING UP BUSINESS IN NIGERIA

Legal Framework for Conducting Business Activities

According to Nigerian investment and promotion commission (1913), all business enterprises must be registered with the Registrar-General of the Corporate Affairs Commission (registrar of companies). Foreign investors wishing to set up business operation in Nigeria should take all steps necessary to obtain local incorporation of the Nigerian branch or subsidiary. Business activities may be undertaken in Nigeria as:

(i)   Private or public limited liability company;

(ii)   Unlimited liability company;

(iii)   Company limited by guarantee;

(iv)   Foreign company (branch or subsidiary of foreign company);

(v)   Partnership/firm;

(vi)   Sole proprietorship;

(vii)   Incorporated trustees;

(viii) Representative office.

The companies and allied matters act and incorporation procedure

The companies and allied matters act, 1990 (the companies act) is the principal law regulating the incorporation of businesses. The administration of the Companies Act is undertaken by the CORPORATE AFFAIRS COMMISSION (CAC), which undertakes the administration of the companies Act, and its functions include:

(i)   The regulation and supervision of the foundation, incorporation, registration, management and winding up of companies;

(ii)   The maintenance of a company's registry;

(iii)   The conduct of investigation into the affairs of any company in the interest of shareholders and the public.

Minimum Share Capital and Disclosures in Memorandum Of Association

The minimum authorized share capital is N10,000 in the case of private companies or N500,000 in the case of public companies. The memorandum of association must state inter-allies that the subscribers "shall take amongst them a total number of shares of a value not less than 25 per cent of the authorized capital and that each subscriber shall write opposite his name the number of shares he takes". However, minimum share capital of N10 million is required for companies needing business permit/NIPC registration, expatriate quota or pioneer status.

The law permits and acknowledges the roles of attorneys and other relevant professionals in facilitating business transactions provided, of course, that this "agency arrangement is disclosed"

Membership of the company – prohibition of trust
The Companies Act prohibits "notice of any trust, express, implied or constructive" and such shall not be entered on the register of members or be receivable by the CAC.

Shares
All categories of company shares to carry one vote. Shares with "weighted" voting right are prohibited. All shares (i.e. whether ordinary or preferential) issued by a company must carry one vote in respect of each share. Consequently, preference shareholders are entitled to receive notices and attend all general meetings of the company and may speak and vote on any resolution before the meeting.

Disclosures to be published in company correspondence and business premises
Every company is obliged to disclose on its letterhead paper used in correspondence, following particulars:

(i)   Name of company/enterprise;

(ii)   Address;

(iii)   Registration/incorporation number;

(iv)   Names of Directors and Alternate Directors (if any)

In addition, the law requires companies/enterprises to ensure that the certificate of registration be displayed in conspicuous positions at their principal and branch offices.

Operation of Foreign Companies in Nigeria

A non-Nigerian may invest and participate in the operation of any enterprise in Nigeria. However, a foreign company wishing to set up business operations in Nigeria should take all steps necessary to obtain local incorporation of the Nigerian branch or subsidiary as a separate entity in Nigeria for that purpose. Until so incorporated, the foreign company may not carry on business in Nigeria or exercise any of the powers of a registered company.

The foreign investors may incorporate a Nigerian branch or subsidiary by giving a power of attorney to a qualified solicitor in Nigeria for this purpose. The incorporation documents in this instance would disclose that the solicitor is merely acting as an "agent" of a "principal" whose names should also appear in the document. The power of attorney should be designed to lapse and the appointed solicitor ceased to function upon the conclusion of all registration formalities.

The locally incorporated branch or subsidiary company must then register with the Nigerian Investment Promotion Commission (NIPC) before commencing formal operations. The new company may also apply to NIPC for other investment approvals (e.g. expatriate quota) and other incentives.

Exemption to the General Rule

Where the exemption from local incorporation is desired, a foreign company may apply in accordance with section 56 of the Companies Act, to the national council of ministers for exemption from incorporating a local subsidiary if such foreign company belongs to one of the following categories:

(a.)   Foreign companies invited to Nigeria by or with the approval of the Federal Government of Nigeria to execute any specified individual project;

(b.)   Foreign companies, which are in Nigeria for the execution of a specific individual loan project on behalf of a donor country or international organization;

(c.)   Engineering consultants and technical experts engaged on any individual specialist project under contract with any of the governments in the federation or any of their agencies or with any other body or person, where such contract has been approved by the federal Government.

The application for exemption from disclosing certain details about the applicant is to be made to the Secretary of the Government of the Federation (SGF). If successful, the request of the applicant is granted upon such terms and conditions, as the Federal Executive Council may think fit.

Foreign Investment Requirement and Protections

Principal laws on foreign investments

The principal laws regulating foreign investment are, the Nigerian Investment Promotion Commission Act No. 16 of 1965 and the Foreign Exchange (Monitoring and Miscellaneous Previsions) Act No. 17 of 1995

Deregulation of equity structure in Nigeria enterprises

Effectively, the Nigerian Enterprises Promotion (Repeal) Act No. 7 of 1995 has abolished any restrictions, in respect of the limits of foreign shareholding, in Nigeria registered/domiciled enterprises. The only enterprises, which are still exempted from free and unrestrained foreign participation, are those involved in:

- ☐ Production of arms and ammunition
- ☐ Production of and dealing in narcotic drugs and psychotropic substances.

The Nigerian investment promotion commission act no. 16, 1995 (NIPC ACT)

This Act established the Nigerian Investment Promotion Commission (NIPC) as the successor to Industrial Development Coordination Committee (IDCC).

Functions of powers

The Nigerian Investment Promotion Commission (NIPC) is an agency of the Federal Government with perpetual succession and a common seal, which is especially established, among other things, to:

(a.) Coordinate, monitor, encourage and provide necessary assistance and guidance for the establishment and operation of enterprises in Nigeria;

(b.) Initiate and support measures which shall enhance the investment climate in Nigeria for both Nigerian and non-Nigerian investors;

(c.) Promote investments in and outside Nigeria through effective promotional means;

(d.) Collect, collate, analyze and disseminate information about investment opportunities and sources of investment capital and advise on request, the availability, chance or suitability of partners in joint-venture project;

(e.) Register and keep records of all enterprises to which the NIPC Act legislation applies;

(f.)   Identify specific projects and invite interested investors for participation in those projects;

(g.)   Initiate, organize and participate in promotional activities such as exhibitions, conferences and seminars for the stimulation of investments;

(h.)   Maintain liaison between investors and ministries, government departments and agencies, institutional lenders and other authorities concerned with investments;

(i.)   Provide and disseminate up-to date information on incentives available to investors;

(j.)   Assist incoming and existing investors by providing support services;

(k.)   Evaluate the impact of the Commission in investment in Nigeria and recommend appropriate remedies and additional incentives;

(l.)   Advice the Federal Government on policy matters, including fiscal measures designed to promote the industrialization of Nigeria or the general development of the economy; and

(m.)   Perform such other functions as are supplementary or incidental to the attainment of the objectives of NIPC Act.

Provision relating to investments

Notable amongst the provisions relating to investment are

the following:

(i.)   A non-Nigerian may invest and participate in the operation of any enterprise in Nigeria;

(ii.)   An enterprise, in which foreign participation is permitted, shall after its incorporation or registration, be registered with NIPC;

(iii.)   A foreign enterprise may buy the shares of any Nigerian enterprise in any convertible foreign currency;

(iv.)   A foreign investor in an approved enterprise is guaranteed unconditional transferability of funds through an authorized dealer, in freely convertible currency of:

a.   Dividends or profits (net of all taxes) attributed to the investment;

b.   Payments in respect of loan servicing where a foreign loan has been obtained; and

c.   The remittance of proceeds (net of all taxes) and other obligations in the event of sale or liquidation of the enterprise or any interest attributable to the investment.

Priority areas of investments

The NIPC issues guidelines and procedure, which specify priority areas of investment and prescribes incentives and benefits, which are in conformity with Government policy.

The preferred sectors for investment are:

1.   Agriculture and Agro-allied;

2.   Solid Minerals;

3.   Tourism;

4.   Information and Communication Technology;

5.   Power and Energy; and

6.   Manufacturing.

Incentives for special investments

For the purpose of promoting identified strategic major investment, the NIPC may in consultation with appropriate Government agencies, negotiate specific incentives package for the promotion of investment

Investment Protection Assurance

The NIPC Act provides that:

(a.)   No enterprise shall be nationalized or expropriated by any government of the federation, and

(b.)   No person who owns, whether wholly or in part, the capital of any enterprise shall be compelled by law to surrender his interest in the capital to any other persons.

There will be no acquisition of an enterprise by the Federal Government unless the acquisition is in the national interest or for a public purpose under a law that makes provision for:

(a.)   Payment of fair and adequate compensation, and

(b.)   A right of access to the courts for the determination of the investor's interest of right and the amount of compensation which he is entitled.

Compensation shall be paid without undue delay and authorization given for its repatriation in convertible currency where applicable.

Apart from the investment guarantee assurances of the NIPC Act, countries are welcome to execute and enter into bilateral Investment Promotion and Protection Agreements (IPPA) with the Nigerian government.

Checklist of steps for establishing new companies in Nigeria with foreign shareholding

Stage A

1.   Establish partners/shareholders and their respective percentage shareholding in the proposed company.

2.   Establish name, initial authorized share capital and main objects of propose company.

3.   Except in instances where the proposed company will be 100% owned by non-resident shareholders – prepare Joint-Venture Agreement between prospective shareholders. The Joint-Venture may specify; inter-alia, mode of subscription by parties, manner of Board Composition, mutually protective quorum for meetings, specify actions which would necessitate shareholders approval by special or

other resolutions.

4. Prepare Memorandum and Articles of Association, incorporating the spirit and intents of the Joint-Venture Agreement.

5. Foreign shareholder may grant a power of attorney to its Solicitors in Nigeria, enabling them to act as its Agents in executing incorporation and other statutory documents pending the registration with NIPC (i.e. formal legal status for foreign branch/subsidiary operations).

6. Conduct a search as to the availability of the proposed company name and, if available, reserve the name with the CAC.

7. Effect payment of stamp duties, CAC filling fees and process and conclude registration of the company as a legal entity.

Stage B

Prepare deeds of Sub-Lease/ Assignment, as may be appropriate, to reflect firm commitment on the part of the newly registered company, to acquire business premises for its proposed operations.

Stage C

An established company proceeds to apply for grant of business permit/NIPC registration, expatriate quota or pioneer status as desired. The following are requirements and fees for respective applications:

1. **Grant of Business Permit/NIPC Registration Requirements:**

i.   Formal application letter to Executive Secretary

ii. Minimum share capital requirement – N10 million

iii. Duly completed NIPC form 1

iv. Certificate of incorporation

v.   CAC's form C02 and C07

vi. Memorandum and Articles of Association

vii. Tax clearance certificate

viii. Certificate of capital importation (for foreign enterprise)

ix. Evidence of acquisition of business premises (Tenancy or Lease Agreement)

x.   Joint venture agreement (where applicable)

xi. Approval from appropriate professional body (where applicable)

xii. Feasibility report.

Fees:

i.   NIPC Form I
        N25,000

ii. Collection of Business Permit Certificate
        N25,000

2. **Expatriate Quota
    Requirements:**

i. Formal application letter to Executive Secretary

ii. Minimum share capital requirement – N10 million

iii. Duly completed NIPC form 1

iv. Certificate of incorporation

v. CAC's form C02 and C07

vi. Memorandum and Articles of Association

vii. Tax clearance certificate

viii. Certificate of capital importation (for foreign enterprise)

ix. Evidence of acquisition of business premises (Tenancy or Lease Agreement)

x. Feasibility report.

xi. Technical service agreement

xii. Evidence that personnel required is not likely to be available in Nigeria

xiii. Training program for Nigerians

xiv. Management succession schedule

xv. Schedule of names, address, qualifications and positions to be occupied by expatriate.

xvi. License permit/certificate from relevant Government Agencies/Department/Ministries/Professional bodies for the operation of the project.

xvii. Evidence of work at hand, its duration and value attached to the contractor(s) if company is engaged in building, civil engineering, constructions, etc.

(original to be presented for sighting).

xviii. Proposed annual salaries to be paid to the expatriates to be recruited indicating designation, names, job description and qualifications (CV and copies of credentials of expatriate are to be attached).

Fees:

i.   Processing fee   N25,000

ii.   Payment for each quota position approved N25,000

3.   Pioneer status incentive

The benefit of a pioneer status certificate is that the holder (i.e. the company) is exempted from payment of tax for a specified number of years (5 years in urban area and seven years in rural area).

Requirements:

i.   Formal application letter to Executive Secretary

ii.   Minimum share capital requirement – N10 million

iii. Duly completed NIPC form 1

iv.   Certificate of incorporation

v.   CAC's form C02 and C07

vi.   Memorandum and Article of Association

vii. Tax clearance certificate

viii. Evidence of acquisition of machinery (form M)

ix.   Evidence of acquisition of business premises (Tenancy or Lease Agreement)

x.   Feasibility report.

xi.   Joint Venture Agreement (where applicable)

xii.   The company must not be more than one year old from commencement of production.

xiii.   Joint venture must attain a minimum qualifying capital expenditure of N5 million.

Fees:

i.   NIPC Form II   N20,000

ii.   Processing fee   N50,000

iii.   Collection of approval letter   N30,000

iv.   Application for extension   free

v.   Approval of pioneer status extension N50,000

        These fees are as at 2014, it can be reviewed forward anytime.

4.   Technical service agreement

        This is a form of technical co-operation agreement in which a party will agree to offer technical services to a company for the payment of a fee.

        Details and terms of such agreements are normally worked out between the parties involved but such agreements should be registered with the National Office for Technology Acquisition and Promotion (NOTAP).

Stage D

1. Having obtained the requisite NIPC approvals, the non-resident shareholders must act with dispatch to import its foreign equity holding in the company. To ensure prompt importation of the foreign equity components, the NIPC may register company but defer approval for Expatriate Quota and Pioneer Status and other applicable investment incentives, until evidence of capital importation is produced.

2. After obtaining Certificate of Importation from the bank, the NIPC is to be notified of this fact with the supporting documentation, in order for it to resume processing of pending approvals that might have been deferred on such ground.

3. As soon as expatriate quota position are granted and the respective individuals to fill the quota positions are recruited, the company must embark on steps to obtain work permit and residency status for the expatriate employees and their accompanying spouses and children (if any).

Meaning Of 'NIPC Registration' and 'Expatriate Quota'

NIPC Registration confers permanent authorization for the local operation of business with foreign investments either as branch/subsidiary of a foreign company or otherwise.

Expatriate quota is the official permit to a company; conveying permission for the company to employ individual expatriates to specifically approved job designations, and also specifying the permissible duration of such employment.

The expatriate quota forms the basis of work permits for expatriate individuals employed (whose qualifications must fulfil the criteria established for the particular quota position). Expatriate quota positions are usually granted for 2-3 years subject to renewal, except in cases where companies qualify for and are granted "PUR" Quota (i.e. Permanent Until Renewed) position.

The Current Regulation on the Appointment of Foreign Directors

The promoters of business ventures in Nigeria are free to appoint directors of their choice, either foreign or Nigerian, and the directors may be resident or non-resident. The application to the NIPC must reflect the names of the proposed Nigerian and foreign directors (with an indication of resident or non-resident directors). The Registration Certificate consequently issued following such application usually reflects the respective names of the proprietors of the company, as well as the directors representing each proprietor or co-proprietor.

Payments of foreign directors' fee are remittable in the same manner as dividends accruing to the foreign company. However, since such fees are taxed at source (5% as a withholding tax), each foreign director's fees are remittable subject to satisfactory evidence that the taxable amounts on such fees have been paid

115

REFERENCES

Adeyinka, O. (1987): Nigerian Business and Economic Environment. A paper presented at National Workshop organised by the National Directorate of Employment, Lagos, 1st - 5th June, 1987.

Asoga-Allen, K. (2012) A handout prepared for 100 level degree students of Ekiti State University, Michael Otedola College of Primary Education Campus, Noforija-Epe.

Asoga-Allen, K. (2013) A handout prepared for 200 level degree students of Ekiti State University, Michael Otedola College of Primary Education Campus, Noforija-Epe.

Edewor, J. O. (1987). Adapting Technology to Local Conditions. A paper presented at the National Workshop organised by the National Directorate of Employment, University of Lagos, Akoka, Lagos. 1st - 5th June, 1987.

Ladipo, J. K. (1987) My Experience as a Nigerian Businessman. A paper presented at the National Workshop organised by the National Directorate of Employment, University of Lagos, Akoka, Lagos 1st - 5th June, 1987.

Nigerian Entreprises Promiotion Act No 7 of 1995. Download from www.nigeriahcottawaaca/other-services/investment-opportunities.

The Companies and Allied Matters (1990) Download from www.nigerialaw.org/companiesandalliedmattersact.html

Index

A

C

D

E

F

G

H

I

J

L

M